The Facilitator's Guide to the Galaxy

A Companion for Undertaking

Group Conversation, Collaboration & Consensus

Elisabeth White

Copyright © 2019 Elisabeth White

All rights reserved.

ISBN: 9780578569413
ISBN-13: 978-0-578-56941-3

Table of Contents

Preface 0
The Journey Begins 1
The Facilitator 2
Techniques of the Trade 4
Across the Galaxy 6
Facilitation Toolkit 7
Purpose-Driven Agenda 8
The End in Sight 9
Reflect & Adjust 10
Facilitator Retrospective 11
Methods to the Madness 12
Lean Coffee – *The What* 14
Lean Coffee – *The How* 15
Lean Coffee Retrospective 17
Campfire – *The What* 18
Campfire – *The How* 19
Campfire Retrospective 22
Open Space – *The What* 23
Open Space – *The How* 25
Open Space Follow Up 29
Open Space Retrospective 30
World Café – *The What* 30
World Café – *The How* 32
World Café Mural 35
World Café Retrospective 36
The Journey's End (or Beginning) 36
References 38

In honor of the Founding Mother of Agile Facilitation, **Jean Tabaka**

ACKNOWLEDGEMENTS

Infinite gratitude to Travis Dent, Will Fehringer, Doug Huffman, Jim Lambert, Jesse Pearlman, and Parker Stephenson for dedicating countless hours of their precious time to engage in conversation, collaboration, and consensus with me. And many thanks to the Agile community for seeking better ways of communicating by continuously *reflecting* and *adjusting*.

Live it, love it, be it, do it!

Preface

"Don't Panic." –Douglas Adams, The Hitchhiker's Guide to the Galaxy

Time is precious and isn't limitless. People across the galaxy spend hours engaged in conversations; some meaningful, others meaningless. Meaningless hours of conversation cannot be recouped or replenished. However, those hours can be learned from and adjustments can be made—with a little help.

Facilitators have the unique opportunity of creating environments where meaningful conversation, collaboration, and consensus are achievable. Facilitators provide flexible structure, safe space, and guidance that keeps conversations flowing toward a desired outcome. The goal is to create a thriving environment for meaningful conversation to flourish. Like a symphony conductor, a Facilitator masterfully brings dynamic characteristics and personalities together to rhythmically orchestrate conversation. But there is an art form to facilitation, an art form that perhaps has been taught through hushed whispers and tribal knowledge.

Until now! For those who have self-selected or been "voluntold" to serve in this critical, state-altering role, *The Facilitator's Guide to the Galaxy* sets out to provide the necessary provisions and basic knowledge needed to effectively create environments where meaningful conversation, collaboration, and consensus are achievable—despite the event, the participants, and/or content. From novice to expert, there's bound to be provisions for any facilitation journey.

The Journey Begins

"The journey of a thousand miles begins with one step." –Lao Tzu

A discussion topic has been selected. A date and time have been set. A location has been determined. A group of diverse and dynamic people have come together. The conversation will start soon. 3…2…1… Facilitation liftoff!

But wait… Where's the Facilitator? Before any conversation launches into the great unknown, someone must navigate the galaxy. The power of group conversation comes from the journey participants embark upon to arrive at a desired destination. Without guidance and proper support, conversation can quickly turn to chaos, and the journey becomes a nightmare with no destination in sight. Conversations lacking facilitation rarely have a successful launch and often drift into the black abyss. The result is time-sucking meetings and meaningless conversation.

Set the conversation up for success! Identify a Facilitator and allow him/her enough time to prepare for the journey. Depending on the type of conversation, the Facilitator may need a few hours or a few days to properly prepare. Provide the Facilitator with the necessary information he/she will need to pack the right provisions.

It's ==critical== that the Facilitator not be expected to participate or serve as a content contributor. The Facilitator must have the ability to focus on the environment, the direction and flow of the conversation, and the desired destination. By taking this first crucial step, the conversation already has a higher likelihood of success because someone will be dedicated to guiding the journey and avoiding pitfalls.

One step down, a thousand more to go! Facilitation itself is a journey. A Facilitator needs practice and exposure to a plethora of conversations before he/she can safely navigate the galaxy. Be patient with the Facilitator and realize that their sheer presence has already increased the value of the conversation. Every twist and turn are a learning opportunity for the participants and the Facilitator.

The Facilitator

"The wise facilitator speaks rarely and briefly,
teaching more through being than doing." –The Tao Te Ching

In theory, facilitation seems simple, straightforward, and doable by most. In practice, facilitation is not for the faint of heart; it requires a high degree of organizational skills, verbal and written finesse, and fine-tuned listening. The art form of facilitation calls on the ability to blend into an environment, as if the Facilitator was naturally meant to be there. Successful Facilitators work tirelessly so participants can contribute effortlessly.

So, what are some characteristics of a successful Facilitator?

- **Selfless** – The success of the Facilitator is not measured by his/her contributions but rather the output of the facilitation.
- **Relational** – The Facilitator has an uncanny ability to connect with diverse and dynamic individuals and sincerely cares about the well-being of all participants.
- **Unbiased** – The Facilitator avoids prejudice and judgment, focusing on the overall outcome instead of one individual or data point.
- **Prepared** – The Facilitator has properly planned and organized the event by proactively identifying what will be needed to facilitate the conversation.
- **Flexible** – The Facilitator knows that unexcepted events are sure to happen and can pivot and adjust accordingly.

If the goal is to create a thriving environment for meaningful conversation to flourish, the Facilitator must cultivate and adjust the environment in a healthy and vigorous way. The emphasis is placed on the overall success of the conversation instead of personal contribution.

For this to be possible, the Facilitator:

- **Should *not* be a participant** – It's a conflict of interest for the Facilitator to both contribute to the conversation and maintain the overall environment.
- **Should listen before speaking** – Creating the space needed to promote participation demonstrates the ability to facilitate instead of contributing.
- **Should *not* have a stake in the conversation** – It's easy to slip into contributing if the content is applicable or valuable to the Facilitator.

- **Should be approachable** – Participants should feel comfortable discussing topics with the Facilitator before, during, and after the conversation.
- **Should *not* lose track of time** – Every minute of the conversation deserves attention. Losing track of time could cause the conversation to spin out of control and will likely result in a blown timebox.
- **Should follow up** – Once the conversation has concluded, it's the Facilitator's responsibility to capture takeaways, action items, and ensure participants know next steps (and how to take them).

Techniques of the Trade

"Great dancers are not great because of their technique,
they are great because of their passion." –Martha Graham

Facilitation techniques can be extremely helpful, especially when dealing with difficult content, personalities, and/or surroundings. But the greatest technique a Facilitator can utilize is his/her own passion. Energy, enthusiasm, and a genuine presence in the conversation encourages the participants to remain active and present. It's crucial that the Facilitator portray body language, tone, and volume that best supports the environment.

Establishing a true passion for facilitation is often an acquired taste—it takes time. For some, it comes naturally; like breathing. Until passion fuels the Facilitator, and even once their facilitation is laced with energy, the following techniques can be beneficial in creating and sustaining the right environment for group conversation:

- **Agenda** – Create an agenda for every conversation to clearly outline the purpose of the discussion and key talking points.
- **Participant List** – Acquire a participant list prior to the conversation and try to identify any conversation dominators or silent contributors who may need additional facilitation support.
- **Space Setup** – Determine what type of space will best support the conversation, and ensure the setup provides the technical, writing, walking, standing, and/or seating arrangements needed.
- **Supplies** – Bring any required supplies needed to successfully create the environment for facilitating the conversation.
- **Working Agreements** – Establish any necessary guidelines that will create a safe space, limit distractions, and promote a healthy flow of dialogue for all participants.
- **Timekeeping** – Ensure a clock or timer is nearby and keep track of the minutes.
- **Timeboxing** – Add a timebox to each agenda item by assigning a specific number of minutes that participants will have for dialogue, and track to it (do not exceed the overall time allotted for the event).
- **Parking Lot** – Maintain an area where ideas and/or questions that are potentially off-topic, but still relevant, can be captured for future follow up (or with any remaining time at the end of the conversation).

- **Fidget Toys** – Place pipe cleaners, play dough, or spinners within the space to keep hands busy and minds focused on the conversation.
- **Dot Voting** – Provide participants with small dot stickers that can be used for prioritization and consensus building. It's at the Facilitator's discretion to determine how many votes each participant will be given and when to engage in voting.
- **Visual Facilitation** – Use color and shapes to depict the conversation in addition to written words.

Sample Working Agreements

1. Be on time and end on time.
2. No use of electronics (unless it's an emergency).
3. One voice at a time—avoid speaking over one another.
4. No side conversations or unnecessary disruptions.
5. Be engaged and present—actively contribute.

Sample Timeboxing

1. Kick Off/Opening Remarks – 5 min.
2. Introductions – 30 secs. per participant (5 min.).
3. Topic 1 – 7 min. of discussion, 3 min. of Q&A.
4. Topic 2 – 10 min. of discussion, 5 min. of Q&A.
5. Action Items & Assignees – 7 min.
6. Wrap Up/Closing Remarks – 3 min.

Across the Galaxy

"When it comes to challenging times, I often say,
'If it was easy, someone else would be doing it.'" –Giacomo 'Peldi' Guilizzoni

Distributed conversations have become a part of daily life. It's inevitable that a Facilitator will encounter group conversations where participants are dispersed across the galaxy. When possible, the Facilitator should always encourage face-to-face conversations and avoid unnecessary distance (separated by office walls or building floors). But when space stations are light years apart, face-to-face conversation may simply be impossible.

The environment needed to facilitate these conversations should still utilize the same facilitation techniques and purpose-driven agenda, but the Facilitator should prepare in a slightly unique way. The space and provisions must be virtualized!

The Facilitator must have a virtual presence—he/she should be the first person with working audio and visual capabilities. Hearing and seeing the Facilitator sets the expectation that, despite the distance, all participants will be heard and seen. There must also be a way for the Facilitator to capture key takeaways and action items and share them with the virtual participants (ideally live time).

Provisions for Distributed Conversations:

- **Quiet Surroundings** – There's nothing worse than background noise when facilitating distributed conversations. It's imperative that the Facilitator and all participants eliminate distractions and ambient sound, so the conversation is clear.
- **Virtual Space** – Without white boards and easel pads, the Facilitator will need a virtual environment to guide the conversation. This could be as simple as an online document that can be shared and worked on simultaneously.
- **Audio** – The Facilitator and all participants will need the ability to hear and converse with one another easily and clearly.
- **Visual** – The Facilitator and all participants will need the ability to see one another to create a virtual face-to-face environment.

Facilitation Toolkit

"If you get stuck, draw with a different pen.
Change your tools; it may free your thinking." –Paul Arden

To navigate the galaxy, every Facilitator should have a "Facilitation Toolkit." A Facilitation Toolkit holds all the essential provisions needed to facilitate through a variety of conversations. It should be with a Facilitator at all (facilitation) times to assist with creating the right environment for the conversation. It's important that the Facilitation Toolkit be portable, lightweight, and easy to maneuver. It should also provide multiple colors in its supplies. Participants tend to be visual learners, and color can promote creative thinking.

Consider decorating and naming the Facilitation Toolkit to emphasize its importance and criticality—this is also a way to let the Facilitator's personality shine through. Make sure to check supplies frequently and replenish as needed to prevent any unnecessary last-minute preparation scrambling!

Essential Supplies Inside a Facilitation Toolkit:

- White Board Markers (in 4+ colors)
- White Board Eraser
- Flip Chart Markers (in 4+ colors)
- Sticky Notes (in 4+ colors)
- Fine Point or Regular Markers (in at least one bold color)
- Circle Color-Coding Labels (stickers)
- Name Tents
- Blank Paper
- Painter's Tape (or other easy-to-remove tape)
- Scissors
- Timing Device
- Other supplies the Facilitator finds himself/herself using on a regular basis

Purpose-Driven Agenda

"The secret of your success is determined by your daily agenda." –John C. Maxwell

Before any conversation begins, a baseline understanding of the content needs to be established. To avoid meaningless, time-sucking conversations, an agenda needs to be created. But not just any agenda, a *purpose-driven agenda*. Time is precious. Every minute within a group conversation should have purpose and provide value. The Facilitator will use the purpose-driven agenda as his/her compass, guiding the conversation to its desired destination.

Structure of a Purpose-Driven Agenda:

1. **Date, Time (with time zone, if needed), Location, Directions (if applicable)** – Avoid confusion by providing all the data up front.
2. **Participants** – Both contributors and silent observers:
   - Identify the Facilitator
   - Identify any key speakers
3. **Purpose** – The "why" for the conversation and key talking points that need to be discussed.
4. **Desired Outcome** – If the purpose is realized, what can be achieved throughout the conversation?
5. **Agenda** – Structure and sequencing of the conversation with timeboxes.
6. **Methodology** – The event/session method that will be used for the conversation (if applicable).
7. **Provisions** – Any supplies that will be used during the conversation.
8. **Working Agreements** – Any preestablished guidelines that all participants need to adhere to.

The End in Sight

"To conquer frustration, one must remain intensely focused on the outcome, not the obstacles." –T.F Hodge

During most group conversations, the Facilitator will be the only person able to focus on guiding the participants toward the desired outcome. Not losing sight of why the group set off on the journey in the first place is critical to the success of the conversation. The Facilitator must redirect participants when they've veered off course. But there's a finesse to interruption that a Facilitator will master over time.

Again, the focus for the Facilitator is on creating a thriving environment for group conversation to flourish. Forced disruption can cause the environment to deteriorate rapidly. Instead of abrupt interruption, the Facilitator will use a combination of "leading questions" and consensus building to subtly course-correct the conversation. Leading questions are unbiased in nature and encourage participants to pause and quickly reflect on the conversation. This creates the thinking space needed for the participants to refocus on achieving the desired outcome. These questions are readily available to the Facilitator and can be used at any point within the conversation.

Leading Questions for Facilitation:

1. We have spent "___" minutes on this subject. Are we all in agreement that we should stay focused on this subject, or should we move on?
2. I believe everyone has had the opportunity to contribute to this discussion topic. Are we ready to move on?
3. Real quickly, I'd like to remind the group that our desired outcome is "_____." Are we sure this discussion is helping us achieve that outcome?
4. If today's purpose is "_____," are we in agreement that we're focused on the right discussion topics?
5. We have several items in the parking lot. Are we sure we're focused on the correct outcome? Perhaps we should consider pivoting the conversation to what's most important to the participants?

Reflect & Adjust

"I can't change the direction of the wind, but I can adjust my sails to always reach my destination." –Jimmy Dean

It's mission critical that the Facilitator not become stagnant in his/her facilitation journey. Environments and technology are continuously evolving, which requires the Facilitator to always be learning—facilitation is not a one-stop destination.

Every conversation is an opportunity to learn and improve. It's important that the Facilitator take time after every conversation to reflect on what transpired and identify opportunities to improve and adjust techniques. A retrospective is a great activity that can be lightweight and easy to conduct for self-reflection. It's important for the Facilitator to identify what areas of growth he/she wants to focus on and ensure that the retrospective covers those areas.

The Facilitator should maintain a prioritized backlog of captured action items so that he/she can implement changes or new ideas/techniques as similar, and different, facilitation opportunities are presented. The "Facilitator Retrospective" can be used as a starting point for reflecting and adjusting, or it can be used as a repeatable template.

3 Goals that can be achieved with the Facilitator Retrospective:

1. Capture learning opportunities after every facilitation session.
2. Identify action items for continuous improvement.
3. Track growth patterns and trends throughout the facilitation journey.
   - Avoid stagnation and celebrate growth!

Facilitator Retrospective

WHAT TECHNIQUES WORKED WELL? _____
_____
_____
_____
_____

WHAT MADE THE FACILITATION DIFFICULT? _____
_____
_____
_____
_____

WHAT COULD BE DONE DIFFERENTLY? _____
_____
_____
_____
_____

PRIORITIZED ACTION ITEMS:

   1. _____
   2. _____
   3. _____
   4. _____
   5. _____

Methods to the Madness

"It is common sense to take a method and try it. If it fails, admit it frankly and try another. But above all, try something." –Franklin D. Roosevelt

There are many different methods that can be utilized to facilitate group conversations, depending on the environment that the Facilitator needs to create. The facilitation method can be informal or structured—again, it's up to the Facilitator to understand the purpose, desired outcomes, and agenda to identify the best approach to facilitating the session.

Each facilitation method has different attributes that support conversation, collaboration, and consensus. Sometimes, it's obvious which method should be used, and sometimes, a Facilitator must simply attempt a method and reflect afterward. Facilitation methods can also provide a starting point for the Facilitator. The goal is to enable the Facilitator to be successful in their facilitation role while creating the best possible environment for the group.

There are four essential methods that a Facilitator should be familiar with:

- Lean Coffee
    - Created by Jim Benson and Jeremy Lightsmith and preserved at leancoffee.org
- Campfire
    - Inspired by Roger Schank and Gary Saul Morson's book, *Tell Me a Story: Narrative and Intelligence (Rethinking Theory)*.
- Open Space (Technology)
    - Developed by Harrison Owen and further explored at openspaceworld.org
- World Café
    - Discovered by Juanita Brown and David Isaacs and maintained by the World Café Community Foundation at theworldcafe.com

The best way to learn these methods is to put them into practice. To do so, a Facilitator must know what the facilitation method is, when best to use it, and how to facilitate through it.

The following overviews provide:

- a brief description of each method—*the what.*
- recommendations for facilitating each method—*the how.*
- a retrospective template that can be used to reflect, adjust, and capture action items after completing a facilitation session utilizing each method.
    - It's important to note that further exploration into each facilitation method will increase the depth and breadth of the Facilitator's ability to successfully utilize these methods to their maximum benefit.
    - In-depth information and advanced descriptions for each method can be found at the mentioned sources.

Lean Coffee – *The What*

"Conversation is the most human and humanizing thing that we do." –Sherry Turkle

According to leancofee.org, "Lean Coffee is a structured, but agenda-less meeting. Participants gather, build an agenda, and start talking. Conversations are directed and productive because the agenda for the meeting was democratically generated."

But what does it mean to have an agenda-less meeting that still has an agenda? The goal of Lean Coffee is to eliminate single contributors and any preconceived topics that traditionally would be prepared prior to the session. Lean Coffee aims to address the issue of participants missing out on the opportunity to play an active role in topic choices and discussion. By arriving without an agenda and instead democratically generating it, an environment of early engagement and consensus is created.

Lean Coffee is a wonderful facilitation method for conversation starters, team building, retrospectives, strong/opposing opinions, and/or a change in pace (disrupting stagnate meeting cultures). It's a very lightweight method and has very few guidelines for facilitating, making it a great technique for Facilitators of all levels. Lean Coffee encourages short timeboxes, so the conversation is in a continuous flow. More than one topic may be discussed, depending on how the participants democratically choose to move through the conversation.

It's important to note that Lean Coffee is a highly interactive and visual facilitation method. Lean Coffee utilizes a Kanban Board, stickies, markers, and voting. This can be a difficult technique to conduct remotely unless a virtual environment can be optimized for the method (i.e. digital Kanban Board).

Lean Coffee – *The How*

"Good communication is as stimulating as black coffee, and just as hard." –Anna Spencer

Supplies:

- A Kanban Board with the following workflow states:
    - Backlog
    - In Progress
    - Done
        - The workflow states may be customized to meet the needs of the session.
- Stickies
    - Depending on the session, the color and size of the sticky may or may not be applicable.
- Markers
    - Marker color(s) should be bold so that stickies are easy to see/read by participants.
- Voting mechanism
    - Dot, color, shape, etc. voting may be used to democratically prioritize the conversation.
- Timing device
- Seating (and standing) area around the Kanban Board
- Any additional supplies necessary based on the environment, the participants, and the Facilitator.

Preparation:

- Determine the appropriate timebox, location, and participants prior to the session.
    - The timebox should take into consideration a quick introduction (if participants are unfamiliar with the method and/or one another), topic generation, topic explanation, voting, prioritization, and discussion.
    - Leave time at the end of the session to capture action items!
- Create the Kanban Board prior to participant arrival.
- Have stickies, markers, and voting mechanism ready at each seat to save time.

Facilitation Steps (recommended approach – reflect and adjust as needed):

1. Provide a quick (<2-minute) overview of what the Lean Coffee method is.
2. Provide each participant with stickies and a marker.
3. Set the timer to 5 minutes and allow the participants to write down their desired discussion topics for the session.
4. At the end of the 5 minutes, the Facilitator should encourage each participant to, one-by-one, place their topic stickies in the "Backlog" of the Kanban Board.
   - Participants may wish to provide a high-level overview (<2 minutes) of their topic stickies before returning to their seat.
5. Provide each participant with 3 votes. These votes will be used to prioritize the topic stickies within the "Backlog."
6. Explain to the participants that they may cast all 3 votes on 1 topic sticky, 2 votes on 1 topic sticky and 1 vote on another topic sticky, or 1 vote on 3 topic stickies.
7. Encourage participants to approach the Kanban Board, review the topic stickies, cast their votes, and return to their seats. This should be done as a collective group and not one-by-one.
8. Organize and prioritize the "Backlog" based on the number of votes on each topic sticky.
   - Remove any topic stickies that have no votes.
9. Pull the highest priority from the "Backlog" and place it in the "In Progress" workflow state.
10. Set the timer to X minutes. (This could be 5-10 minutes, depending on the duration of the session and the number of voted topic stickies.)
11. Start the timer and encourage the author of the topic to kick off the conversation.
12. Once the timebox has been met, stop the conversation.
13. Before moving back to the "Backlog," ask the participants if they would like to add 5 minutes to the current topic or if they would like to move on.
    - Use "Roman Voting" to determine if participants want additional time (thumbs up) or if they would like to move on (thumbs down).
14. Either increase the timer to 5 minutes or place the topic sticky in the "Done" workflow state.
15. Repeat steps 9-14 until all voted topic stickies have been discussed or the session timebox has been reached (leaving time for wrap up).
16. Capture action items, assign action takes, and conclude the session!

Lean Coffee Retrospective

WHAT WENT WELL? _____

_____

_____

_____

_____

WHAT WAS DIFFICULT? _____

_____

_____

_____

_____

WHAT COULD BE DONE DIFFERENTLY? _____

_____

_____

_____

_____

PRIORITIZED ACTION ITEMS:

1. _____
2. _____
3. _____
4. _____
5. _____

Campfire – *The What*

"You don't have to say everything to be a light. Sometimes a fire built on a hill will bring interested people to your campfire." –Shannon L. Alder

The Campfire facilitation method is rooted in generations of storytelling around millions of campfires across the galaxy. Inspired by Roger Schank and Gary Saul Morson's book, *Tell Me a Story: Narrative and Intelligence (Rethinking Theory)*, this method encourages reflection of the past through storytelling format to identify lessons learned that can be applied to future activities. The focus is less on current affairs and rather on using historical information to influence future decision making and action items.

Campfires can require a level of vulnerability and trust that not all environments are ready for. It's critical that the Facilitator knows the audience and creates safe space for open dialogue. It's also ==very== important that the Facilitator invites participants to share their stories but does not require it—storytelling often raises emotions that not all participants are ready to confront.

This facilitation method is often used for team building, retrospectives, root cause analysis, and/or less formal environments. Campfires can be highly creative, fun, and upbeat, depending on the topics that are discussed. They can also lead to heavy conversation that may require one-on-one follow up with participants. It's up to the Facilitator to gauge how light or heavy the Campfire should become.

Like Lean Coffee, the Campfire method requires a "Backlog," consensus building, is highly interactive, has only a few strict guidelines, welcomes customizations, and works best with in-person engagement. This facilitation method is ==very== difficult to facilitate virtually. Topics are referred to as logs, and logs are either put on the fire while the conversation is burning or extinguished if the conversation has ended.

Location, time of day, and group size are not crucial to facilitate a successful Campfire, but often times having a replica of a campfire helps set the stage and inspire participants (it can be a simple drawing on a sticky, an empty firepit, or a fire place—burning or otherwise).

Campfire – The How

"Light a campfire and everyone's a storyteller." –John Geddes

Supplies:

- A Kanban Board with the following workflow states:
    - Tinder
    - Burning
    - Extinguished
        - The workflow states may be customized to meet the needs of the session.
- Stickies (aka logs)
    - In honor of the campfire metaphor, orange and yellow stickies add to the atmosphere, but are not required.
- Markers (aka matches)
    - Marker color(s) should be bold so that stickies are easy to see/read by participants.
- Voting mechanism
    - Dot, color, shape, etc. voting may be used to democratically prioritize the conversation.
- Timing device
- Seating area near the Kanban Board
- Campfire, fire pit, or fireplace replica or symbol
- Any additional supplies necessary based on the environment, the participants, and the Facilitator

Preparation:

- Determine the appropriate timebox, location, and participants prior to the session.
    - The timebox should take into consideration a quick introduction (if participants are unfamiliar with the method and/or one another), log chopping, topic explanation, voting, prioritization, and discussion.
    - Leave time at the end of the session to capture action items!
- Create the Kanban Board prior to participant arrival.
- Set up the seating area around the campfire (or whatever will serve as the campfire).

- Have stickies, markers, and voting mechanism ready at each seat to save time.

Facilitation Steps (recommended approach – reflect and adjust as needed):

1. Provide a quick (<2-minute) overview of what the Campfire method is and the importance of providing narratives from the past.
    - Explain the Campfire vernacular:
        - Camper = Participant
        - Log = Sticky note
        - Match = Marker
        - Tinder = Backlog
        - Burning = In Progress
        - Extinguished = Done
    - Conduct optional storytelling atmosphere setting if the Facilitator wishes to get into character.
2. Provide each camper with "logs" and a "match."
3. Set the timer to 5 minutes and allow the campers to write down their desired discussion topics for the session.
4. At the end of the 5 minutes, the Facilitator should encourage each participant to, one-by-one, place their logs in the "Tinder" of the Kanban Board.
    - Campers may wish to provide a high-level overview (<2 minutes) of their logs before returning to their seat.
5. Provide each camper with 3 votes. These votes will be used to prioritize the logs within the "Tinder."
6. Explain to the campers that they may cast all 3 votes on 1 log, 2 votes on 1 log and 1 vote on another log, or 1 vote on 3 logs.
7. Encourage campers to approach the Kanban Board, review the logs, cast their votes, and return to their seats. This should be done as a collective group and not one-by-one.
8. Organize and prioritize the "Tinder" based on the number of votes on each log.
    - Remove any logs that have no votes.
9. Pull the highest priority from the "Tinder" and place it in the "Burning" workflow state.
    - To support the metaphor, the Facilitator should also create an identical log and place it on the campfire and/or campfire symbol in the middle of the seating area.

10. Set the timer to X minutes (This could be 5-10 minutes, depending on the duration of the session and the number of voted logs.)
11. Start the timer and encourage the author of the log to kick off the conversation by telling a personal story (that is at least one day old) that relates to the log.
    - If the author does not feel comfortable sharing a story, then engage the other campers.
12. Encourage campers to build off the first story told by sharing their own stories that relate to the log. The conversation must stay in storytelling format and be reflective of the past.
13. Once the timebox has been met, stop the conversation.
14. Ask the campers if they learned anything about the log based on the stories shared.
    - Keep the discussion to <5 minutes
    - The Facilitator should capture takeaways.
15. Before moving back to the "Tinder," ask the campers if they would like to add 5 minutes to the current burning log or if they would like to move on.
    - Use "Roman Voting" to determine if campers want additional time (thumbs up) or if they would like to move on (thumbs down).
16. Either increase the timer to 5 minutes or place the log in the "Extinguished" workflow state.
    - Don't forget to metaphorically stomp out the identical log in the campfire!
17. Repeat steps 9-15 until all voted logs have been "Extinguished" or the session timebox has been reached (leaving time for wrap up).
18. Capture action items, assign action takers, and conclude the session!

Campfire Retrospective

WHAT WENT WELL? _____

_____

_____

_____

_____

WHAT WAS DIFFICULT? _____

_____

_____

_____

_____

WHAT COULD BE DONE DIFFERENTLY? _____

_____

_____

_____

_____

PRIORITIZED ACTION ITEMS:

1. _____
2. _____
3. _____
4. _____
5. _____

Open Space – The What

"To get real diversity of thought, you need to find the people who genuinely hold different views and invite them into the conversation." –Adam Grant

First developed by Harris Owen, Open Space Technology (also known as Open Space) is a facilitation method that can be particularly impactful with large groups, complex environments of diverse thought and cultures, and can span multiple days. According to openspaceworld.org, "Open Space establishes a marketplace of inquiry, reflection and learning, bringing out the best in both individuals and the whole."

Participants play an active role in their personal engagement and the overall outcome of the session—a desire to move and participate is critical. The Open Space facilitation method combines large group presentation with small breakout sessions. There is an overarching theme or question that is set at the beginning of the session that drives overall conversation and keeps breakout sessions anchored in common discussion.

Unlike Lean Coffee or Campfire, the Open Space facilitation method has explicit guardrails that protect conversations, encourage collaboration, and necessitate consensus building. These guardrails are referred to as "The Four Principles" and "The One Law."

The Four Principles of Open Space:

1. Whoever comes is the right people.
2. Whatever happens is the only thing that could've.
3. When it starts is the right time.
4. When it's over, it's over.

The Law of Two Feet:

- If people find themselves in situations where they are neither learning nor contributing, they are responsible for moving to another place—using their two feet to find a place where their participation is more meaningful.

In conjunction with the outlined guardrails, the Open Space method has basic mechanisms that provide for a successful session. The guidance for each mechanism is lightweight, easily understood, and should be followed. How each mechanism is operationalized is largely up to the Facilitator, along with any input from the participants (although guidance can be found at the cited Open Space sources). With that said, neglecting to operationalize and follow the mechanisms can result in undesirable outcomes and/or chaos across participants and the session.

Open Space Mechanisms:

1. Invitation
2. Circle
3. Bulletin Board (Timetable)
4. Marketplace
5. Iteration
6. Storytelling

The Open Space facilitation method can be somewhat complex until the Principles, Law, and Mechanisms are mastered. Open Space requires robust preparation and high-engagement facilitation throughout the session. The Facilitator should engage one or more Co-Facilitators to support the method so the desired outcome(s) may be achieved.

Open Space – *The How*

"The biggest mistake is believing there is one right way to listen, to talk, to have a conversation—or a relationship." –Deborah Tannen

Supplies:

- Suitable venue
    - Attendance can range between 5-1,500 people. Make sure the venue will properly accommodate a large group and small breakout sessions.
    - Microphones and speakers may be required based on room and audience sizes.
- Colored 8x11 paper
    - Only to be used in the large group area.
- Stickies
    - It's best to use paper during the large group activities and stickies during breakout sessions.
- Markers
    - Marker color(s) should be bold so that paper stickies are easy to see/read by participants.
- Flipcharts for each breakout area
- Timing device (one for each Facilitator)
- Painter's tape to create the Bulletin Board
- The Bulletin Board
    - Wall space divided into sections using painter's tape to capture time slots and associated topics.
- Large circular seating area, breakout areas, wall space within the large group area for the Bulletin Board
- Any additional supplies necessary based on the environment, the participants, and the Facilitator/Co-Facilitators

Preparation:

- Determine the appropriate timebox, location, participants, and number of Facilitators prior to the session.

- The timebox should take into consideration:
    - The number of participants (more people = more topics).
    - Providing 10-15 minutes of explanation of the mechanics and flow of the method.
    - Reviewing the Principles, Law, and Mechanisms.
    - Directions for finding breakout areas.
    - Time at the end of the session for participants to share reflections from their overall experience.
- Set up the large group area.
    - Check audio equipment (if applicable).
    - Post the "The Four Principles" and "The One Law" on a wall using flipchart paper.
    - Set up chairs in a circular seating arrangement.
    - Place colored paper and markers on the ground, in the center of the circle.
    - Identify an area within the circle for participants to present their topics during the Marketplace.
    - Create the Bulletin Board on a blank wall.
        - Timetable with breakout areas (vertical columns) and timeslots (horizontal rows).
        - Assign a Facilitator to each breakout area.
    - Post the "Reflection/Storytelling" on a wall using flipchart paper.
- Designate at least one Facilitator to assist with the Bulletin Board.
    - This Facilitator will assist with placement of topics within breakout areas and timeslots to avoid overcrowding spaces.
- Designate at least one Facilitator to keep a steady rhythm for the Marketplace.
    - This Facilitator will assist with supplies within the circle and keeping participants timely in their Marketplace contributions.
- Have stickies, markers, and flipcharts ready at each breakout area.

Facilitation Steps (recommended approach – reflect and adjust as needed):

1. Provide the *Invitation*.
    - Set the theme or question that will guide the overall conversation and topic ideation.
    - This should be included in any pre-communication to participants.
2. Set the *Circle*.

- Encourage participants to sit within the circle to show that they're "in" the conversation.
3. Showcase the *Bulletin Board*.
    - Review the use of the Bulletin Board and provide instructions on how to engage the Bulletin Board Facilitator.
4. Open the *Marketplace*.
    - Encourage participants to take 5 minutes to reflect over the *Invitation*.
    - After reflection, invite the participants to head to the middle of the circle to fill out a piece of paper with a topic for discussion.
        o One topic per piece of paper.
    - As participants begin to generate topics, have them present the topics to the group (form a line, or two lines, and allow participants 30 seconds-1 minute to share).
        o Topic generation and presentation may be conducted simultaneously or staggered.
    - After a participant shares an idea, direct them to the Bulletin Board to find a breakout area and timeslot for their topic.
        o Presentations should continue while participants make their way to the Bulletin Board.
    - Guide participants back to the circle after posting the topic on the Bulletin Board to listen to presentations and/or generate additional topics.
5. Close the *Marketplace*.
    - Participants may go back through the line with additional topics until the Bulletin Board is full.
    - Once the Bulletin Board is full, halt topic generation and request participants to take their seats within the circle.
6. Kick Off the *Iterations*.
    - Before allowing participants to review the Bulletin Board and select the topics they wish to discuss, explain how the breakout sessions will work.
    - Let the topic owners (participants that generated the topics) know that they will serve as the conversation starter during the breakout session.
    - Let the participants know how long the timebox is for breakout sessions.
    - Identify the Facilitators associated with each breakout session.
    - Release the participants to review the Bulletin Board and find their breakout areas.

7. Activities during the *Iterations*.
    - It's at the discretion of each topic owner to utilize their session as they see fit. It could be a presentation, Q&A, open dialogue, or any other technique that best encourages the conversation.
    - The Facilitator within each breakout area may assist the topic owner and/or the participants as needed.
    - The Facilitator within each breakout area should capture key takeaways and action items to bring to Storytelling.
    - Breakout session participants may also capture takeaways and action items to contribute to Storytelling.
    - At the end of the breakout session timebox, Facilitators will release their participants back to the large group area.
    - Participants will select a new topic and head to their next breakout area.
    - After the last breakout session, participants will head back to the large group area for Storytelling.
8. Facilitate *Storytelling*.
    - Once all participants have returned to the circle, encourage participants to read what they provided in the Storytelling flipchart. Keep the read-outs to 2-5 minutes.
    - Make sure Facilitators have adequately captured all necessary follow-up items that can be communicated to the participants after the Open Space.
    - After Storytelling has been completed, conclude the Open Space.
9. Follow Up.
    - Provide communication to all participants (including Facilitators) with themes, key takeaways, and prioritized action items with action takers immediately after the session (or within 24 hours).
    - Use the provided template for follow up or create something that best suits the participants.

Open Space Follow Up

WHAT WAS THE *INVITATION?* _____
_____
_____
_____
_____

WHAT WERE THE COMMON THEMES ACROSS TOPICS/BREAKOUT SESSIONS? _____
_____
_____
_____
_____

WHAT WERE THE KEY TAKEAWAYS FROM STORYTELLING? _____
_____
_____
_____
_____

PRIORITIZED ACTION ITEMS & IDENTFIED ACTION TAKERS:

1. _____
2. _____
3. _____
4. _____
5. _____

Open Space Retrospective

WHAT WENT WELL? _____

_____

_____

_____

_____

WHAT WAS DIFFICULT? _____

_____

_____

_____

_____

WHAT COULD BE DONE DIFFERENTLY? _____

_____

_____

_____

_____

PRIORITIZED ACTION ITEMS:

1. _____
2. _____
3. _____
4. _____
5. _____

World Café – The What

"When café life thrives, talk is a shared limberness of the mind that improves appetite for conversation: an adequate sentence maker is then made good, a good one excellent, an excellent one extraordinary." –Vivian Gornick

The World Café facilitation method creates a traditional café atmosphere that ignites colorful and visual conversation. Like Open Space, World Café is a great facilitation method for large, diverse groups. It's also a great method for visual learners and creative/artistic participants.

The World Café Community Foundation states that, "World Café is an easy-to-use method for creating a living network of collaborative dialogue around questions that matter in service to real work." The goal of World Café is to have progressive conversation and collaboration across 3+ rounds of dialogue to inspire a café atmosphere. The World Café facilitation method utilizes the Seven Design Principles as guidelines:

1. Set the Context
2. Create Hospitable Space
3. Explore Questions that Matter
4. Encourage Everyone's Contribution
5. Connect Diverse Perspectives
6. Listen Together for Patterns and Insights
7. Share Collective Discoveries

The Facilitator should be familiar with all seven principles prior to scheduling or facilitating the session. Although not nearly as intensive as the Open Space method, there is still preparation and flow to the World Café method that is required for a successful participant experience. Depending on the size of group that will be engaging in the session, Co-Facilitators may be necessary to achieve the desired outcome(s).

World Café – *The How*

*"I'd much rather hang out in a café.
That's where things are really happening." –Joe Sacco*

Supplies:

- Suitable venue
  - Attendance can range between 5-500+ people. Make sure the venue will properly accommodate a large, open area.
  - Microphones and speakers may be required based on room and audience size.
- Round café tables that seat 5
  - Other shaped tables will work as long they only seat 5 people.
- Butcher block paper (or similar large sheets of paper)
- Marker sets in multiple colors for each table
- Medium/Large sticky pads for each table
- Flipchart for the *Mural*
- Side table with café-like pastries, appetizers, teas, and coffees
  - Optional, but greatly assists in establishing the atmosphere
- Timing device
- Any additional supplies necessary based on the environment, the participants, and the Facilitator

Preparation:

- Determine the appropriate timebox, location, and participants prior to the session.
  - The timebox should take into consideration:
    - Providing 10-15 minutes of explanation of the mechanics and flow of the method.
    - Reviewing the Seven Design Principles.
    - Directions for rotating through the tables.
    - Time at the end of the session for participants to share reflections from their overall experience.

- The Lead Facilitator will serve as the Café Host. The Café Host ensures that the Seven Design Principles are being adhered to and that there's proper flow through the progressive conversations.
- The Café Host should gather "Questions that Matter" prior to the session to properly prepare the participants once the session has started. If there is more than one question, then the questions need to be prioritized.
  - Trying to gather the questions or prioritize them at the beginning of the session can be challenging and detract from the atmosphere.
- The Café Host may designate a Facilitator to serve as the Table Host at each table, or participants may self-select at the time of the session (this is at the discretion of the Café Host but should be decided prior to the session so Co-Facilitators are clear on role and expectations).
- Create the Mural using flipchart paper and post it on a wall within the venue.
  - The Mural will capture themes and key takeaways from all the café tables.
- Place the butcher block paper (or equivalent) on the café tables like tablecloths.
- Place a set of markers and a medium/large sticky note pad on each café table.

Facilitation Steps (recommended approach – reflect and adjust as needed):

1. Welcome participants to the café, and request that they find a seat at one of the café tables.
   - Introduce the Table Hosts, if they have been pre-determined.
2. Provide an overview of what the World Café method is.
3. Review the Seven Design Principles.
4. Read the first (or only) "Question that Matters" out loud to the café.
5. Set the timer to 10-20 minutes (based on number of questions and overall timebox).
6. Start the timer and encourage participants to start drawing or writing their thoughts, ideas, follow-up questions etc. that correspond to the announced question (directly on the tablecloths).
   - The Table Host should encourage dialogue across the table.
7. Once the timer is met, stop the conversation across the café.
8. Ask that each table capture key findings and takeaways on a medium/large sticky note.
   - Make sure the Table Host collects the sticky note and holds onto it until the end of the session.
9. Request that the participants travel clockwise or counterclockwise to the nearest café table.

- Keep a constant flow in the same direction.
- If Table Hosts were not predetermined, make sure that one participant stays at their first café table and remains there for the duration of the session.

10. After the traveling participants arrive at their next café table, encourage the Table Host to provide a quick overview of the conversation that was had during the first round.
11. Set and start the timer again. This time, encourage traveling participants to build off the conversation at their new table, instead of generating new thoughts, etc.
12. Once the timer is met, stop the conversation across the café.
13. Repeat steps 8-10 for the third and final round.
14. Once the timer is met for the third round, stop the conversation and send the traveling participants back to their first café table.
15. Set the timer for 5-10 minutes (based on remaining time).
16. Start the timer and encourage participants to reflect over the three conversations woven into one at their café tables.
    - Table Hosts may assist with facilitating the discussion at each table.
17. Once the timer is met, stop the conversation and request that the Table Hosts take the medium/large stickies to populate the Mural.
18. The Café Host will review the Mural with the café participants.
19. If there are additional "Questions that Matter," repeat steps 4-18.
    - Make sure to replace the current tablecloths with blank ones and create a new Mural.
20. If there are no other "Questions that Matter," conclude the session.
21. Share/Send the Mural(s) to the participants immediately after the session (or within 24 hours).
    - Use the provided template or create something that best suits the participants.

World Café Mural

WHAT WAS/WERE THE *QUESTIONS THAT MATTER?* _____
_____
_____
_____
_____

WHAT WERE THE COMMON THEMES ACROSS THE CAFÉ TABLES? _____
_____
_____
_____
_____

WHAT WERE THE KEY TAKEAWAYS FROM EACH CAFÉ TABLE? _____
_____
_____
_____
_____

PRIORITIZED ACTION ITEMS & IDENTFIED ACTION TAKERS:

1. _____
2. _____
3. _____
4. _____
5. _____

World Café Retrospective

WHAT WENT WELL? _____
_____
_____
_____
_____

WHAT WAS DIFFICULT? _____
_____
_____
_____
_____

WHAT COULD BE DONE DIFFERENTLY? _____
_____
_____
_____
_____

PRIORITIZED ACTION ITEMS:

1. _____
2. _____
3. _____
4. _____
5. _____

The Journey's End (or Beginning)

*"Enjoy the journey and try to get better every day.
And don't lose the passion and the love for what you do." –Nadia Comaneci*

There's no better time than the present to set off on a facilitation journey or reflect and adjust the current path of exploration!

Parting Inspiration:

- Experiment! Don't be afraid to try new techniques and reflect on what works and what doesn't work. ==Reflect and adjust!==
- Find time to explore! New ideas, technologies, techniques, methods, tools, and galaxies are being discovered all the time. Be a part of the exploration and discovery!
- Be open to feedback! Feedback is crucial to continuous learning and growth. Never shy away from an opportunity to learn and improve. A destination can cause stagnation—don't let the journey die!
- Grow and expand the facilitation community! Find time and outlets to share learnings, key takeaways, and success stories to strengthen the network of Facilitators!
- Have fun! Although facilitation is critical for group conversation, collaboration, and consensus, it should still be an enjoyable experience for participants and a journey worth traveling for the Facilitator.

References

1. Brown, Juanita and David Isaacs, with the World Café Community of Practice. 2005. *The World Café Book: Shaping Our Futures Through Conversations that Matter.* San Francisco: Berrett-Koehler Publishers.

2. Leancoffee.org

3. Herman, Michael. 1998. "Working in Open Space: A Guided Tour." openspaceworld.org/wp2/explore/guided-tour/

4. Owen, Harrison. 2008. *Open Space Technology: A User's Guide.* San Francisco: Berrett-Koehler Publishers.

5. Owen, Harrison. "Opening Space for Emerging Order." openspaceworld.com/emergent_order.htm

6. Schank, Roger and Gary Saul Morson. 1995. *Tell Me a Story: Narrative and Intelligence (Rethinking Theory).* Evanston, IL: Northwestern University Press.

7. The World Café Community Foundation, theworldcafe.com

ABOUT THE AUTHOR

Born and raised in the great state of Colorado (GO Broncos!), **Elisabeth White** is an Agile (and coffee) aficionado with a passion for people and transformation. She's spent the last decade guiding organizations on incredible Agile journeys—focusing on continuous improvements within *Culture, People, Processes, and Tooling*. Elisabeth is a Coach by profession, Facilitator by trade, and an Agilist at heart.

She's attempting to save the world, one Agile journey at a time!

Made in the USA
San Bernardino,
CA